Hummingbirds

A PORTRAIT OF THE ANIMAL WORLD

Hal H. Wyss

TODTRI

This book was designed and produced by
TODTRI Book Publishers
P.O. Box 572, New York, NY 10116-0572
FAX: (212) 695-6984
e-mail: info@todtri.com

Printed and bound in Singapore

ISBN 1-57717-134-9

Author: Hal H. Wyss

Publisher: Robert M. Tod
Senior Editor: Edward Douglas
Book Designer: Mark Weinberg
Typesetting: Command-O, NYC

Visit us on the web!
www.todtri.com

PHOTO CREDITS
Photographer/Page Number

Peter Arnold Inc.
R, Hansen-Peter 18
Guenther Ziesler 15

Jeff Foott Productions
Jeff Foott, 3, 47 (top), 48
Windland Rice 28 (top), 40–41

Joe McDonald 5, 29, 35, 39, 51, 52, 53 (top & bottom), 61, 62, 64 (top), 68–69

Photo Researchers Inc.
Toni Angermayer 43
Steve Bentsen 60 (left)
Nick Bergkessel 16, 26, 46, 50
Paulo Bonino 12, 17 (top right)
Gregory C. Dimijian 67, 70 (bottom)
Jerry L. Ferrara 55
Kenneth Fink 11 (top)
S.C. Fried 31, 49
Francois Gohier 14, 27
Woodrow Goodpaster 36 (top)
G.C. Kelley 4, 8–9, 11 (bottom),19, 20, 23, 28 (bottom), 33, 43 (top), 44, 47 (bottom), 56–57
Stephen J. Krasemann 32 (bottom), 42
Robert Lee 21
S. Maslowski 32 (top)
Anthony Mercieca 10, 24–25, 38, 59 (bottom), 63 (top & bottom), 64 (bottom) 65, 69, 70 (top), 71
Gary Retherford 22
J.H. Robinson 13
Jany Sauvanet 17 (top left and bottom), 66
Karl Weidmann 6
Kent Wood 7
Jim Zipp 45

Picture Perfect
John Warden 58

Gary Pollock 34

Tom Stack & Associates
John Cancalosi 30
Wendy Shattil/Bob Rozinski 36 (bottom), 37 (top), 59 (top)

Connie Toops 37 (bottom), 54, 60 (right)

INTRODUCTION

Costa's hummingbird was named after Louis Marie Pantaleon Costa, a nineteenth-century French naturalist and collector of hummingbird specimens.

Where I live in southern Michigan and, in fact, in that large region east of the Mississippi and north of the Gulf Coast where a substantial portion of the United States population lives, hummingbirds are not abundant. There is only a single species, the ruby-throated hummingbird, and it does not assemble in conspicuous flocks. Still, I am always surprised when a visiting relative, friend, or student says that the ruby-throat I just pointed out at one of our feeders or on our red salvia is the first hummingbird he or she has ever seen.

Hummingbirds are neither rare nor difficult to observe, and the fact that there is only one species where most of us live does not mean that they represent a small group of birds. Ornithologists have various classification systems, especially now that taxonomists are making discoveries showing that birds once thought to be closely related probably aren't and those thought to be only distant cousins are really close relatives. But they all agree that hummingbirds are a major distinctive group, possibly aligned with swifts, and that there are between 315 and 350 species of hummingbirds in two large classes, true hummingbirds and hermits.

Hummingbirds are found only in North, South, and Central America and nearby islands. The largest class of birds confined to the New World is comprised of flycatchers, but hummingbirds are next, making up about 10 percent of all New World bird species. A single species, the rufous hummingbird, breeds in southeastern Alaska as far north as the sixtieth parallel, and another breeds at the southern tip of South America in Tierra Del Fuego near the fifty-fifth parallel south. Between these breeding boundaries, species are distributed in a classic bell curve peaking at the equator.

In fact, more than half of all hummingbird species may be found in the small country of Ecuador, and more than 90 percent spend most or part of each year between the Tropic of Cancer and the Tropic of Capricorn. Sixteen species occur regularly in all of North America north of Mexico, compared to more than fifty in tiny Costa Rica.

Most people think of hummingbirds as among the most beautiful and intriguing of creatures. In the mass gift catalogs that arrive shortly before Christmas each year, they receive attention and space equal to that devoted to loons, wolves, eagles, and whales. Yet since they were unknown to Europeans before the voyages of Columbus, they are missing from classical and Renaissance art and literature. Other large families of birds (hawks, owls, gulls, thrushes, and so forth) are found in Europe as well as in the Americas. So, although Shakespeare mentions a virtual aviary of birds in his plays and poetry, he left out hummingbirds. And Romantic poets Keats and Shelley, not having been brought up where hummingbirds live, extolled the beauty of such relatively drab birds as nightingales and skylarks.

Unfortunately, there was one kind of attention that Europeans did begin paying to hummingbirds in the second half of the nineteenth century. Because of their small size and bright, iridescent colors, hummingbirds are often referred to metaphorically as flying jewels. In the nineteenth century their skins were literally incorporated into pieces of jewelry and other fashion accessories. Stuffed hummingbirds were used almost as commonly as egret feathers to decorate women's hats or handbags and with similar results. That is, as the fashion industry drove the snowy egret to the brink of extinction, so did it drastically reduce the population of several hummingbird species; it may even have been responsible for some extinctions. Millions of hummingbird skins were sold in Europe between 1850 and 1910. Thankfully, hummingbirds are no longer hunted for their feathers, but a few are still killed and ground into powder in Latin America as an ingredient in love potions.

The hummingbird is the smallest of all birds. Even the giant hummingbird (an oxymoron akin to "jumbo shrimp") of the South American Andes, which is twice as large as any North American hummingbird, is only a little more than 8 inches (20.3 centimeters) in length and weighs in at a hefty 20 grams (about 5/8 ounce). The tiny male Cuban bee hummingbird may weigh less than two grams (6/100 ounce, about the same as a dime), and at 2 1/4 inches (5.7 centimeters) long is the smallest of all warm-blooded creatures. And several others—including the green and white hummingbird of Peru and the calliope

hummingbird of the southwestern United States—are only slightly larger.

A typical ruby-throated hummingbird weighs about 2.8 to 3 grams (9/100 to 1/10 ounce). To make up a pound of them would require 150 hummingbirds. Balancing a single bald eagle on one side of a scale would take an amazing 2,100 hummingbirds on the other side. We often use shrimp as a metaphor for smallness, but one middle-sized shrimp (thirty to a pound) weighs the same as five garden-variety hummingbirds.

Smallness is not the only way in which hummingbirds are creatures of extremes. Hummingbirds have both the highest metabolism and the highest heart rate found among birds. At times, especially in desert or tropical habitats, this may cause them to overheat, but since they have no sweat glands they must disperse excess heat by panting and spreading their feathers to promote air cooling. Not surprisingly they have the fewest feathers of any bird, but because of the very small surface area on a hummingbird's body, those few feathers are arranged more densely than those of any other bird. They have the largest ratio of skin surface to body mass, a condition that makes them especially vulnerable to heat loss, but they have no down.

When hovering, hummingbirds' wings beat substantially faster than those of other birds, and hummingbirds are the only birds that can hover efficiently for long periods, fly backward, and, when alarmed, fly upside down for short distances. Although they feed only during the day, hummingbirds eat more frequently than other birds and consume a higher percentage of their body weight in high-energy food. Their feathers are the most iridescent, although varying degrees of iridescence are not unusual among many kinds of birds including the common pigeon. Although they are small, they are unusually pugnacious in defending territories, and they are sexually more promiscuous than most birds. Males often mate with several females in a single season and females may produce more than one brood sired by different males in the same summer.

This book explores hummingbird physiology and behavior and provides some tips on ways to attract these fascinating birds and to observe them in their natural habitats.

Here two hummers feed on one of the many red flowers available in Madera Canyon, Arizona.

HUMMINGBIRD PHYSIOLOGY

Most of the more remarkable physical characteristics of hummingbirds are in some way related to their small size. Temperature control, for example, is a major problem for a warm-blooded creature of such tiny body mass, particularly considering that hummingbirds may live at high altitudes, where the temperature drops below freezing most nights; they may also forage on cactus flowers in the Sonoran Desert, where temperatures of 120°F (49°C) are not uncommon. The way in which most hummingbirds feed—hovering in front of their food source rather than perching—requires the expenditure of immense amounts of energy. Hummingbirds must consume large quantities of high-energy food, usually nectar but sometimes tree sap, which has a sugar content of 20 percent or higher. And their extraordinarily high rate of metabolism permits them to utilize this food rapidly. Their resting heart rate of 600 beats per minute may soar to over a thousand when they are hovering.

Of course, the ability to feed by hovering is itself made possible by some unusual physical adaptations. The wings of hummingbirds are proportionately longer, narrower, and stiffer than those of most other small birds; they are sometimes compared to oars. Fully 30 percent of a typical hummingbird's body weight is contained in the breast muscles that move these wings. Also, many hummingbirds have uniquely shaped bills that have evolved to enable the birds to feed on specific kinds of flowers. Others, including all the hummingbirds found in the United States, are generalists; they feed on a variety of flowers and have medium sized, straight, or slightly curved bills.

Hummingbird feathers are the most densely packed of those of any bird, but, even though heat loss is a serious problem for many hummingbirds, there is no under layer of down; even infant hummingbirds are naked or have only a hint of down that disappears as they

FOLLOWING PAGE: Here the stiff-oarlike wing, so specific to hummingbirds, is clearly evident in this photograph of a broad-billed hummingbird about to feed in Madera Canyon, Arizona.

Since hummingbirds can collect nectar from flowers high in the air with no perch before them for landing, there is no competition with other nectar-feeding creatures.

The ability of hummingbirds to feed while hovering is one of their characteristics that is most fascinating. While feeding, they are virtually flying, and beat their wings faster than those of other birds.

Metabolism and Feeding Adaptations

As a general rule, metabolism becomes more rapid as body mass decreases. Smaller birds like chickadees and wrens have metabolic rates ten times as high as chickens, and hummingbirds have the most rapid metabolic rates of all birds. In addition to size, another contributing factor is the very high energy consumption caused by their manner of feeding. Most birds and insects that utilize nectar perch on or in front of the nectar source and are virtually at rest while they feed. This, of course, limits the selection of flowers available to them as food sources. Hummingbirds, and a very few other creatures such as the hummingbird moth, are able to collect nectar without landing. They are thus able to utilize many flowers not available to perching nectar feeders, but this carries a very high cost in energy expenditure.

Nectar is a marvelously efficient energy source. Hummingbirds are able to extract and convert into energy more than 95 percent of the sugar in nectar. On average, a hummingbird experiencing normal weather conditions and pursuing its normal activities consumes about 50 to 75 percent of its body weight in sugar each day. Since the sugar makes up about 20 to 25 percent of the nectar of flowers most frequented by hummingbirds, the actual weight of the nectar is about two and a half to three times the bird's weight. Some flowers have nectar with much higher sugar concentrations, but hummingbirds shy away from these, probably because the higher concentrations make the nectar more gummy, which causes problems for the hummingbird's bill and tongue.

But hummingbirds also need protein, which they can't get from flowers. So they eat a substantial number of small insects or spiders each day, and some species have even been observed raiding spiders' webs to collect trapped insects. Usually, however, they catch living fruit flies or gnats, although larger varieties of hummingbirds may take insects as large as wasps and beetles. They do not, as was once thought, use their tongues the way frogs do to snatch insects out of the air. Rather, they catch them with their bills or lap up crawling insects from flowers.

For birders, and especially hummingbird enthusiasts, the tropics offer an exciting opportunity to observe such specimens as this splendid male Jamaican streamer-tail.

mature. The distinguishing characteristic of some specialized feathers found on many species of hummingbirds is their brilliant iridescence, the brightest of all birds. Male hummingbirds position themselves to display these feathers when they are attempting to attract a female. In some species, males also sport long or oddly shaped tail feathers that they also display during courtship. The tail feathers of the Jamaican streamertail, for example, are three times as long as the rest of the bird.

Protein sources appear to make up about 25 percent of a hummingbird's diet, but several conditions may cause this to vary. Birds preparing to migrate gorge themselves on nectar to build up energy reserves for the long journey; they reduce their insect intake at this time. Conversely, females producing eggs need more protein and increase the proportion of insects and spiders they consume. Newborn hummingbirds have the highest need for protein. In the remarkable growth spurt during their first three weeks of life, their body mass increases tenfold, from about 1/100 ounce to 1/10 ounce (.3 to 3 grams). The mother supplies them primarily with insects and with only a small amount of nectar.

Hummingbirds have evolved bills and tongues especially suited for harvesting flower nectar. Generalists—the group to which all the hummingbirds regularly found in the United States belong—feed on a variety of flowers; their bills tend to be narrow and relatively long (as long as the bird's head to about one and a half times as long), and either straight or curved downward slightly. The length of the bill permits them to reach nectar located deep within tubular or trumpet-shaped blossoms,

In addition to brilliant plumage, many male hummingbirds, especially among the tropical species, have long tail feathers that catch the notice of the opposite sex. This red-tailed comet, a native of the northern Andes, is one of many examples.

Though nectar is a major part of their diet, hummingbirds also need a source of protein. To obtain this vital nutrient, they feed on spiders, fruit flies, gnats, and other small insects.

11

sources that are beyond the reach of bees, butterflies, and most moths.

Latin American species have a wide range of bill sizes and shapes because they are more likely to be specialists feeding on only one or two kinds of blossoms. As a rule, exotic bill shapes coincide with the shapes of the flowers upon which hummingbirds depend for food, an adaptation that only works in the tropics, where one species of flower can bloom throughout the year. The sword-billed hummingbird of the Andes, for example, has developed a bill of four to five inches, nearly as long as its entire body. It feeds almost exclusively on two kinds of mountain flowers whose nectar source is extremely deep. Sicklebills, as their name implies, have sickle-shaped bills that curve dramatically downward, making

these birds well-adapted for feeding on flowers with curved blooms. If a sicklebill is holding its head level, the tip of its bill will point to the ground. A few Latin American hummingbirds have very short, sharply pointed bills but still feed on large blossoms with deep nectar sources. They accomplish this by piercing the flower wall and stealing the nectar. That is, they feed but do not benefit the plant by transferring its pollen to another blossom.

Since hummingbirds see clearly through the entire color spectrum but bees cannot see red, flowers frequented and pollinated primarily by hummingbirds are often red. However, some of the flowers most attractive to them such as columbines and jewelweed are not red. Hummingbirds have taste buds and quickly learn to distinguish flowers with the proper

This splendid hummer, feeding on an orchid, is the Brazilian ruby hummingbird, a native of the central and Atlantic provinces of Brazil.

With their long bills—sometimes longer than their heads—hummingbirds are able to probe into flowers to obtain nectar that is out of reach to bees, butterflies, and other insects.

Color, not fragrance, is important to hummingbirds in choosing flowers to feed on. Hummers can discern color through the entire spectrum, and though they are fond of red, other colors attract them as well.

The bill of this white-bearded hermit is perfectly adapted for feeding on a **Heliconia rostrata** *in Peru's Tambopata Reserve.*

sugar content in their nectar from those that are too rich or too watery. Flowers frequented by hummingbirds usually do not have much fragrance, since, unlike bees, hummingbirds do not depend on smell to locate food sources.

Hummingbirds extract nectar by lapping it up with the forked tips of their long tongues, which are usually about as long as the bill but may be extended to twice that length. The tips of the tongue are often fringed and contain

central grooves or channels. The bird pushes its tongue into the nectar source and fills the grooves, then retracts the tongue, closes its bill, and pushes the tongue forward using the closed bill to squeeze out the nectar. The principle is the same as that of the familiar sponge mop.

By this method the birds typically consume about a half a teaspoon or ten calories of sugar daily. This is roughly equivalent to a human eating 150,000 to 200,000 calories each day, akin to devouring fifty to seventy-five pounds of pure granulated sugar. Given its body mass, a hummingbird consumes proportionately the same amount of sugar in a day that a person in a sugar-rich environment like that of the United States consumes in a year.

Inevitably there are times when not enough nectar can be found or when unusual weather conditions increase a hummingbird's energy needs beyond the point where it can satisfy them. This is a creature so highly charged and energetic that it is constantly living on the edge of disaster, either from temperature stress or lack of nectar. To counterbalance this, nature has provided the hummingbird with a safety mechanism, the ability to go into a state known as torpor, a kind of brief hibernation that permits them to reduce drastically their rate of metabolism and their heartbeat and to lower their temperature by twenty or more degrees. Not all species have this capacity, but it is prevalent among those that migrate to temperate climates subject to cold snaps and among those living high up in the Andes. North American hummingbirds are among those that experience this condition.

When they enter a state of torpor, hummingbirds reduce their rate of metabolism to the point that they may burn only one-twentieth of the energy they would normally consume. Their body temperature drops by as much as twenty degrees, although those living at altitudes where temperatures often drop below freezing at night seem to have a built in thermostat to halt their temperature drop and increase their metabolism at a certain point. Their heartbeat—an amazing 1,000 to 1,200 beats per minute when feeding or defending their territory and about 600 beats per minute at rest—plummets to between 50 and 150 beats per minute in torpor.

This feeding Plan-alto hermit is aided, not only by his penetrating bill, but by his long, forked tongue which can be extended to lap up the nectar of any blossom.

Hummingbirds are the only birds capable of conserving energy by entering torpor. The mechanism that triggers it is somewhat complicated and is not entirely understood. Often only some of the hummingbirds with the ability to enter torpor actually do, while others experience normal sleep. A reasonable conclusion seems to be that hummingbirds enter torpor when they have not accumulated sufficient energy supplies to withstand a chilly night or when they are trying to store energy prior to migration. Arousal from torpor requires several minutes, during which the bird shivers and fidgets, but it quickly returns to a normal state of activity. In torpor they are so lethargic that they have often been thought dead; early Spanish explorers called them "resurrection birds" because of their apparent ability to come back from the hereafter.

The violet-capped wood nymph prefers the scrub country and forests of eastern Brazil.

Exotic bill shapes have evolved in some hummingbirds species to exploit the particular flowers available in their local habitat. This rufous-breasted hummingbird in French Guyana is a good example of this adaptation.

17

Flight Adaptations

Although it is difficult to argue with the theory that birds evolved from dinosaurs and that feathers evolved from reptilian scales, the evolutionary path from the giant lizards of the Cretaceous period to the miniscule bee hummingbird must have been long and convoluted indeed. Hummingbirds may have the fewest feathers of all birds, but because of their tiny body surface area, they also have the highest feather density.

Bird wings are analogous to the arms and hands of human beings. Assuming a chicken wing to be reasonably typical, the large single bone that attaches to the body is similar to a person's upper arm; the paired middle bones are like the forearm; and the narrow end portion coincides with the hand. In most birds the three wing sections are roughly equal in size, or the forearm section is somewhat longer than the other two. Wings thus structured are flexible, a characteristic required for the constant small adjustments made by soaring birds like vultures and gulls. Hummingbirds do not soar, and their very unusual wing structures are quite different from birds that do. They have very small upper arms and forearms, and the hand portion makes up three-quarters of the entire wing. The result is a long, stiff, oarlike wing that can pivot but not bend very much.

Hummingbirds are known to be superb fliers, their wings beating so rapidly they become a blur as the little birds perform maneuvers impossible for other birds. Surprisingly, however, when hummingbirds are flying forward

The sleek, efficient design of the hummingbird's wings and body is here captured in this stop-action photograph of a blue-throated hummingbird in flight.

High-speed photography has been important in documenting and studying the mechanics of flight used by hummingbirds.

Long, narrow, stiff wings make possible the amazing flying powers of hummingbirds. Their breast muscles, consisting of 30 percent of their body weight, provide the strength to propel themselves through the air.

rather than hovering, their wings don't beat very rapidly. In level flight a ruby-throated hummingbird beats its wings about twenty times a second, compared to twenty-five times a second for the substantially larger chickadee. When hovering, however, the ruby-throat's wing beats increase to about seventy per second, and that's where the blur and familiar buzzing sound set in. Also, middle-sized hummingbirds are only capable of sustaining forward flight at about twenty-five miles an hour or slightly faster. At times hummingbirds seem

to move so rapidly that it is difficult to follow their progress, but that is partly an illusion. In a race they would be soundly beaten by a horse and, of course, by most other birds. Their reputation for speed comes from the fact that small bodies in motion appear to move faster than larger bodies.

High-speed camera studies have shown that hummingbirds vary their wing strokes in order to fly forward, hover, or move backward. They fly forward like other birds by making powerful strokes backward and downward with their

wings to push the air behind them, then trimming their wings to reduce drag as they move them forward. In hovering, they pivot their wings so that the forward edge is higher as the wing is moved forward but the trailing edge is higher during the backward stroke; this creates a figure-eight pattern not unlike that formed by the hands of a swimmer treading water. In hovering, both the forward stroke and the backward stroke are power strokes, whereas other birds and hummingbirds flying forward develop power only during the backward stroke.

All birds that fly have large breast muscles to provide power for moving the wings. Typically, however, only the muscles that push the wing backward—the usual power stroke—are enlarged, and the breast muscles make up about 12 to 15 percent of the bird's mass. In hummingbirds the muscles that move the wing backward and the ones that move it forward are both highly developed and about equal; they account for 30 percent of the weight of the bird.

Hummingbirds can fly forward, backward, hover, and even fly upside down for brief periods. This astonishing agility gives them also the ability to perform brilliant aerial displays in courtship and when threatened.

Iridescence

Among the characteristics most often associated with hummingbirds is the brilliance and magical shimmering of their feathers. Many birds have some degree of iridescence, from the incredible resplendent quetzal of Central America to the ordinary pigeon of Central Park, but it is something of a trademark for hummingbirds. This does not mean that all hummingbirds have it or are even very colorful; the hermits of South and Central America account for twenty-nine species whose plumage is hardly more eyecatching than that of North American sparrows. Although the United States has only sixteen resident species, those species include some very colorful hummingbirds with very iridescent feathers.

Color in birds and other creatures is, for the most part, a matter of reflection. The surface of the creature is covered with pigments that reflect certain colors and absorb others. However, color may also be imparted by refraction (the bending of light rays), in which case the color will appear to shimmer and perhaps even change as the relative positions of the

FOLLOWING PAGE: *Here is a clear and detailed view of the underside of a hummingbird's wing, showing the smallness of the muscle and bone area in relation to the lighter feathered area.*

Unlike other birds, hummers are not protected by an undercoat of down. However, their feathers are densely packed over their bodies—to retain body heat— and in most cases, are brilliantly iridescent.

Anna's hummingbird males are known for their long. steep, spectacular dives and aerial displays. Common along America's West Coast, they are noted for the iridescent patch on the crown and throat.

viewer, the source of illumination, and the object viewed shift. The throat of a ruby-throated hummingbird, for instance, appears to be black when viewed from the side, with the viewer facing the sun. The same throat, seen from the front with the sun behind the viewer, gleams a brilliant red. Many humming-birds have iridescent feathers (usually green) on their backs, heads, or tails that shimmer but do not appear to change color. Here the iridescence is omnidirectional and not espe-cially strong.

The gorget, or throat area, of some male hummingbirds—including all North American species except the violet-crowned humming-bird—may be otherwise unnoticeable and yet appear absolutely dazzling if seen in the prop-er light from the proper angle. In some species, like the Calliope hummingbird, the iridescent feathers are restricted to the throat and alter-nate with ordinary monochromatic feathers. In others, like the Cuban emerald, deeply iri-descent feathers cover the entire breast area. This type of iridescence, which is both bril-liant and monodirectional, allows a male bird to display for its intended mate without attracting attention from any predators out-side the very limited range of iridescence. It is caused by a peculiar feather arrangement unique to hummingbirds. Throat feathers overlap like roof shingles; the inner two-thirds of each feather is covered by other feathers and has no particular optical characteristics. The outer third, however, has an arrangement of microscopic oval refracting structures called platelets. These are layered in varying depths and contain air pockets of varying sizes that allow for differing refractive indices. The result is a combination of refraction and reflection that produces iridescent throat patches rang-ing all the way through the visible spectrum from violet to red.

This ruby-throated hummingbird hovers in the air to sample the nectar of pink corabells. A lucky photographer was able to capture this scene in his backyard in Cleveland, Ohio.

Iridescence is caused by both refraction and reflection of light. Some humming-birds are dull in appearance, while others, like this brilliantly iridescent rufous-tailed hummingbird, are quite dazzling.

Hummingbirds distinguish themselves not just by the apparent swiftness of their flight, but by the noises they make in the air. This Calliope hummingbird will make a loud, cricketlike trilling sound while flying.

The iridescent gorget, or throat area, of this male Costa's hummingbird will be displayed to lure and attract a female during the courtship ritual.

The characteristic violet-blue crown and gorget of the male Costa's hummingbird is quite prominent and used in display to maintain territorial rights over an important feeding area.

HUMMINGBIRD BEHAVIOR

The order to which hummingbirds and swifts have been traditionally assigned is Apodiformes, which means "footless." Early observers believed that these birds literally had no feet and spent their entire lives airborne. Hummingbirds do of course have both legs and feet, but these are small and fragile and used only for perching; hummingbirds do not walk.

Many aspects of hummingbird behavior are notoriously difficulty to study. Obviously they are too small to be fitted with radios to track their movements, and banding, which has met with limited success, is a very delicate business, practiced by only a few experts. The bands themselves are tiny, are invisible on flying birds, and are very difficult to detect from more than a few inches away on perched birds. Occasionally a previously banded bird will be recaptured, but this usually occurs at the same location where the bird was originally banded. In migratory species this confirms that the bird has found its way home after a long journey, but it provides no data on the route or the length of the journey. Only rarely are birds recovered more than a hundred miles from where they were first banded.

Migration routes cannot be confirmed by direct observation but must be deduced by reports and observations of particular species appearing at approximately the same locations at approximately the same time each year. Even when they are settled into their summer or winter territories, the degree to which hummingbirds wander is open to speculation. Still, most of the more credible information related to hummingbird behavior comes from systematic observations of birds made where the birds have established feeding or nesting territories. In North America this is seasonal, but many South American and Central American species spend their entire lives within a few miles of where they were hatched.

The white-chested emerald hummingbird, with its rich iridescent green plumage, is one of many tropical species, outstanding for their brilliance of color.

The magnificent hummingbird can commonly be found in the mountains of southeastern and central Arizona during the summer. For the winter, it migrates to Mexico and more southerly regions.

If there is a female in the vicinity, this perching male ruby-throated hummingbird will make a series of display dives to attract her attention. Actual mating is typically very brief.

a few minutes; copulation is completed in a few seconds.

The entire mating ritual from display to separation lasts only a few moments. The male performs a spectacular flight display in hopes of impressing a female while she sits docilely on a low branch or plant stem to watch. He climbs into the heights, then power dives until he passes her just above ground level; then he climbs again and repeats the performance. Most male hummingbirds' flights are a series of U shapes with the female at the lowest point. Variations include shallower flights like that of the tiny Calliope hummingbird, whose mating flight is often described as pendulum-like, and complete loop-the-loops performed most often in the United States by the rufous hummingbird. Sometimes males engage in "shuttle flying," whereby they fly horizontally back and forth in front of the female, trying to keep their brilliant gorget feathers aimed in her direction while the sun is at the female's back.

If the female is receptive, the male will mount her for a few seconds; on rare occasions the couple may engage in a short tandem

Mating

Some of the best observational information on hummingbird behavior has to do with their reproductive life, because once a female building a nest has been located, she can be depended upon to stay put until the nesting cycle is complete. Hummingbirds decidedly do not mate for life. Among the most promiscuous of birds, male and female hummingbirds usually come together only to mate and that only very briefly. Courtship may last for

This close-up of the gorget of a male rufous hummingbird shows the brilliant iridescent plumage of the throat feathers that appears to be most important in attracting females for mating.

The exquisite plumage of this male broad-billed hummingbird will enable him to attract a mate. Males may mate with several females during the course of the mating season.

flight. Very soon, however, the male will depart. The same male may impregnate several females during the breeding season, and if a female has a second brood, it will be sired by a male different from the one that sired the first brood.

After mating, the entire reproductive cycle of the hummingbird is performed by the female. She may have already constructed or begun constructing a nest, or she may begin just after mating. Unaided, she builds a tiny but (for most hummingbird species) carefully constructed and secure nest of plant fibers and moss bound together and attached to a small limb by silk taken from spider webs. Often compared to thimbles, teaspoons, or walnut shells, hummingbird nests are round, cup-shaped, and less than two inches (5 centimeters) in diameter.

Hummingbirds typically lay two eggs, each about as big as a navy bean. They carefully incubate them until they hatch in twelve to eighteen days. As soon as the eggs have hatched into minuscule infants that are little more than a head attached to a digestive system, the female begins a frantic course of gathering nectar for energy and small spiders and insects for protein to feed her offspring. She does the actual feeding by inserting her bill into the bill of the infant and pumping in the nourishment. Considering the length and narrowness of an adult hummingbird's bill, it often looks as if the newborn is in danger of being skewered.

Hummingbird chicks develop rapidly and fledge quickly, but even within a single species the fledging period varies a good deal. Ruby-throated hummingbirds, for example, usually leave the nest about three weeks after hatching. However, fledging may take as little as two weeks or as long as a month. There seems to be no correlation between the time infants spend in the nest and the weather conditions or abundance of food. However, some ornithologists suggest that fledging may be prolonged if the adult female has to travel long distances to procure nectar and insects, and shortened if food supplies are close at hand. After the infants have left the nest, they may continue to be fed by the mother for a few days up to a few weeks, depending on the food supplies available in their vicinity.

This black-chinned female is patiently incubating her eggs, a process that will take 12 to 18 days. Soon after mating, she built the nest in which her chicks will be hatched and raised.

After mating, the female hummingbird is totally responsible for brooding and raising the young. After they hatch, she feeds her chicks a mixed diet of nectar and small insects.

Hummingbird chicks develop very rapidly. Within three weeks of hatching they are ready to leave the nest. These ruby-throated chicks are exercising their wings in preparation for departure.

Newly hatched hummingbird chicks are extremely fragile and covered only with a small coating of down. They must be gently fed and cared for in the first days of life.

Hummingbird nests are remarkably small. They are round, cup-shaped, and measure less than 2 inches (5 cm) in diameter. The eggs they contain are roughly the size of common white beans.

These fledged chicks may soon leave their nest. But even after they do, they will still be fed by their mother for a short period of time.

Territoriality

In some but certainly not all hummingbird species, males and sometimes even females establish and defend territories. Territorial behavior is associated primarily with males in most kinds of birds, but since male hummingbirds take no part in rearing young, nesting females may also establish territories. The degree to which species exhibit territorial behavior seems to be related to their physical appearance and to their manner of feeding. As a rule, the more brightly colored the species, the more aggressive the behavior, and often it is remarkably aggressive, especially considering how small these birds are. They will dive bomb not only other hummingbirds but also other kinds of birds, butterflies, cats, and even people. Hawks, owls, and crows have been driven away by three-inch-long (7.6-centimeter) rufous hummingbirds, who often gang up on intruders.

Females usually defend territories when they are constructing nests and incubating eggs but not after the eggs hatch, at which point they need to expend all their energy providing food and care to their brood. Males may establish and defend territories throughout the time they spend at their summering or wintering ground. Birds that do this are usually general feeders, not specialists, and they block out a territory large enough to contain sufficient flowers to fulfill their daily nectar requirements. Sometimes particularly rich tropical trees may be divided into several male hummingbird territories.

In the American Southwest, the century plant has dependably rich nectar and is a favorite of the rufous hummingbird. Since these plants grow as tall as eighteen feet, a single plant may comprise the entire territory of a male rufous, who between visits to its flowers, will sit at the very top and survey his

FOLLOWING PAGE: This rufous hummingbird is perched for a rest on a tree in Jackson, Wyoming. It may migrate as far north as southeastern Alaska for the breeding season.

The magnificent hummingbird is fairly large, measuring about 5 inches (12.5 cm). It shares its range with another large hummer, the blue-throated hummingbird.

The Lucifer hummingbird is noted for its dependence on the agave, or century plant, and for its prominent downcurved bill. This species is found in the most southerly portions of the western United States.

Though the smallest of all North American hummingbirds, the Calliope hummingbird migrates over the immense distance between Mexico and western Canada each year.

domain. People have found that they can attract rufous hummingbirds by filling one of their feeders with a slightly richer mixture of sugar water and placing that feeder several feet higher than the others to imitate the tall perch of the century plant.

In northern regions, ruby-throated and rufous hummingbirds sometimes establish territories around sap-bearing trees in the early spring, later moving to an area with flowers. Feeders also may become the focal point of hummingbirds' territories. Territorial birds usually start each day by feeding around the periphery of their territories and gradually work their way toward the center. In this way they have a smaller area to defend later in the day when interlopers are more active; also, defending a large territory requires a quickness only achieved by birds not carrying a heavy load of nectar. Later in the day, the

birds need to eat more to build up energy for the night, so they pull in their defense boundaries accordingly.

Drab-colored hummingbirds seem able to slip unnoticed into other birds' territories and thus are usually not territorial. Hummingbirds that specialize on only a few species of flowers are also not territorial. Their style of feeding is called traplining, because each day their feeding flight is a large circle analogous to that traditionally run by fur trappers. Since they are continually on the move and cover long distances, they are out of sight of many of their food sources at any given time and have no way of defending them. Trapliners tend to live in the tropics, where some species of flowers bloom year round. The hummingbirds spend their entire lives making laps through these flowers and never move far from where they hatched.

Male humming-
birds defend
their feeding
areas, while
females defend
their nests during
the time that
their eggs are
incubating. It is
not uncommon
for several hum-
mingbirds to
gang together
to drive away
a large intruder.

Though the
green violet-
eared humming-
bird can some-
times be seen
in the western
United States,
its preferred
habitats can be
found in Bolivia
and Mexico.

Migration

Hummingbirds are largely equatorial, and like other equatorial land birds, most of them are nonmigratory. The few species that do migrate move from the tropics to temperate zones to nest, some going north and some going south. All the species found regularly in the United States are migratory, although there are some permanent colonies of Allen's, Anna's, and Costa's hummingbirds in southern California. It is not fully understood what evolutionary advantage these tiny birds gain by subjecting themselves to the rigors of migration when they obviously could remain near the equator with the other three hundred hummingbird species, but, most obviously, there are many nectar-rich flowers in temperate zones and much less competition for that food.

Little is known about the migration routes of those hummingbirds that nest at the bottom of South America, but they may migrate up to 1,500 miles (2,413 kilometers) from Tierra Del Fuego to central Chile. In North America both the rufous and the ruby-throated hummingbird are known to travel more than 2,000 miles (3,218 kilometers) each fall and each spring, and some rufous hummingbirds that nest in Alaska cover twice that distance.

Migration routes are affected by the availability of nectar and may not be the same in each direction. Rufous hummingbirds beginning their northward trek in the spring tend to stay west of the Rockies near the Pacific coast. In the fall they drift eastward to take advantage of late wildflowers blooming on the Front Range and continue their return trip to Mexico along the eastern slope of the mountains. In recent years a small but growing group of rufous hummingbirds has flown eastward to the Gulf Coast and passed the winter there, about a thousand miles east of where one would expect them to be.

Although rufous hummingbirds have the longest migration loop, ruby-throated hummingbirds make the longest and most incredible single migratory leap of any hummingbird. Each year many of them fly nonstop across the Gulf of Mexico to the Yucatan Peninsula, a single sustained flight of more than 500 miles (805 kilometers). They work their way south to the Florida panhandle, spend several days gorging themselves on nectar, and then confidently head off into the void. In the days before the flight, their body weight increases by as much as 50 percent, all of it in energy-rich fat. Usually they wait to begin the long flight until a cold front has passed to provide at least a cross wind, if not a tail wind. A ruby-throated hummingbird has a top flight speed of between 25 and 30 miles an hour (40–48

Anna's humming-birds, unlike some other North American species, do not travel a great deal. They may move about their home ranges, looking for fresh food supplies, but they do not migrate over great distances.

Rufous hummingbirds are noted for the extensiveness of their migratory travels. They may fly as far as 2,000 miles each fall and each spring in search of nectar-rich feeding grounds.

kilometers), but it can't average that rate. So, although it is impossible to track a hummingbird's flight across the gulf, estimates are that it lasts between thirty and forty-five hours, an incredible feat for a creature that weighs 1/9 ounce (3 grams) and ordinarily never flies at night. Legend persists that ruby-throated hummingbirds get across the gulf by riding on the backs of geese and swans. However charming this notion, the fact is that the hummingbirds arrive in Mexico earlier than do the geese and swans.

In spring, surprisingly, the northernmost hummingbirds—rufous in the west and ruby-throats in the east—often appear on their summering grounds before very many flowers are in evidence. One wonders how creatures that must consume something like half their weight in sugar each day just to survive can stake out territories where only crocuses and a handful of daffodils are visible and where nighttime temperatures may still fall below freezing. But they can be seen buzzing among the aspens and birches of Michigan's Upper Peninsula in early May when the trees are just beginning to bud and more of the ground is covered by patches of old snow than by new plant growth.

The explanation is that nature produces more than one kind of sugar water, and

hummingbirds do well on tree sap while they are waiting for early flowers to bloom. Perhaps the factor that most influences the time at which hummingbirds arrive is the migration of sapsuckers. Because hummingbirds are not equipped to chisel holes in trees to make sap flow, they follow sapsuckers and move in after the sapsuckers have had their fill. Also, sap flows freely in early spring from branches that have been broken by winter ice storms.

The mortality rate for migrating hummingbirds is thought to be very high, but no one knows exactly how high. In fact, we still

Distinctive for its violet-blue crown and elongated gorget, the male Costa's hummingbird is also noted for its spectacular aerial displays.

The ruby-throated hummingbird is common throughout the eastern portions of the United States and Canada. This particular specimen is enjoying a plant known as beebalm.

The black-chinned hummingbird breeds in western North America as far north as British Columbia. It can be found during the winter in Mexico.

haven't been able to figure out the average life span for these jewels of nature. One banded broad-tailed hummingbird was recaptured alive twelve years later, the current record. Others have been recaptured seven or eight years after first being banded, and hummingbirds in captivity have lived ten years. The consensus is that the North American hummingbirds able survive the rigors of migration probably have an average life span of four or five years.

With their high metabolism and their vulnerability to temperature extremes and food shortages, it is likely that more die from natural causes than from predation. Observers have seen hummingbirds killed by an unlikely assortment of predators including hawks, cats, frogs, spiders, and praying mantises. Perhaps a few small raptors like the South American bat falcon include a significant proportion of hummingbirds in their diet, but most hummingbirds are simply too little and too quick to be reasonable targets for predators. The energy required to catch one of these little acrobats is generally greater than the energy available in its two or three grams of flesh.

The migratory range of the broad-tailed hummingbird reaches from Idaho and Wyoming down to Mexico and Guatemala. The stress on these migratory birds is high, and many do not survive their long journeys.

The deeply colored sparkling violet-ear hummingbird is a native of Ecuador. Typically, tropical hummingbirds do not migrate, since their food supply is constant year round.

ATTRACTING AND OBSERVING HUMMINGBIRDS

In these days of deeply divisive environmental controversies, happily hummingbirds represent one of the least controversial kinds of creatures found in the wild. Unlike spotted owls, they do not threaten the livelihood of lumberjacks; unlike golden eagles and grizzly bears, they do not harm livestock. They do not leave unsightly and smelly reminders of their presence in parks and on golf courses like Canada geese. They are seldom involved in devastating collisions with cars as are white-tailed deer. They share with the monarch butterfly and the Arctic grayling the distinction of being thought of favorably by almost everybody who notices them at all. Simply put, hummingbirds are at once both as harmless and as delightful as it is possible for a creature to be.

Not surprisingly, more and more people are no longer satisfied with stained-glass hummingbirds hanging in their kitchen windows and colorful representations on their T-shirts and tea towels. They are anxious to get to know these beautiful "jewels of nature." There are, of course, essentially only two ways to get to know hummingbirds. The first and perhaps best is to lure them into your vicinity, assuming that you live somewhere where that is practical. It is feasible in most rural, small-town, and suburban neighborhoods in the United States because hummingbirds are found in all states except Hawaii. However, because most northern and eastern states are home to only one or at most two or three species, people wishing to meet several kinds of hummingbirds have to travel to the southwest or to Latin America.

A ruby-throated hummingbird feeding on a trumpet creeper is a sight that can be seen in any backyard that features flowers most attractive to hummingbirds.

True aficionados, this author included, do both. We put up feeders, plant lots of flowers and shrubs known to be hummingbird attracters, and talk to our travel agents about nature tours to Arizona and South and Central America.

Feeding

Hummingbird feeders are both readily available and inexpensive. With a little thought and a bit of patience, they almost always work. Patience is crucial because, unlike the seed feeders put up for finches and chickadees, hummingbird feeders often go for weeks without being visited by anything other than ants and bees. And while a sunflower or niger seed feeder can be hung up and forgotten until the birds start eating, hummingbird feeders require a good deal of attention. Hummingbirds are not interested in sugar water that has fermented or is fouled by the bodies of dead ants. In some locations, such as southeastern Arizona with its wide

Feeders should be placed out of direct sunlight and away from strong winds. Red is, of course, the preferred color, though yellow feeders are sometimes used as well.

Simple sugar water is perhaps the best food to place in a hummingbird feeder. However, feeders of this type require a great deal of care and maintenance to make sure that the food is always fresh and attractive to the birds.

variety of species or Colorado with its huge population of broad-tailed hummingbirds, feeders are emptied by their intended customers long before they can become repulsive. Where I live in Michigan, the two or three ruby-throated hummingbirds that daintily sample my offerings barely lower the fluid level before it is time for me to empty, carefully clean, and refill the feeders.

Most commercially available feeders work well when properly maintained. They have a reservoir for several ounces of sugar water, three or four feeding ports, bee guards, and enough red trim to catch the eye of passing hummingbirds. Commercial imitation nectar is available, but ordinary granulated sugar will do. Everyone seems to agree that clear sugar water is preferable to commercial mixtures colored with red food dye; even tiny amounts of extraneous chemicals can cause harm to a creature this small, and the red coloring on the feeder itself is sufficient to catch the bird's attention.

The recommended mixture is four parts water to one part sugar. Mix the nectar in a saucepan and bring it to a boil briefly to kill bacteria and mold. Keep a small supply of reserve nectar in the refrigerator to avoid having to mix it every time the feeders need replenishing. Depending on how hot the weather is and how frequently birds are reducing the supply, plan on cleaning and refilling the feeders every two to five days.

The kind of plantings a gardener should select to attract hummingbirds depends on location, but a good general rule is that the plants should include species with have tubular or trumpet-shaped flowers; species that bloom at various times or, ideally, all season; and varieties that come in red. In southern Michigan, tall red salvia and nicotiana—which are attractive to ruby-throated hummingbirds—are so easy to grow that they are virtually foolproof, and they bloom from May to October or whenever the first frost occurs. Such perennials as coral bells, columbines, monarda or bee balm, and jewelweed also seem irresistible, but they bloom for only two or three weeks.

Trumpet vine is especially attractive. Its flowers are so large that hummingbirds must probe more deeply than usual to reach the nectar, a process they find uncomfortable because they can't see approaching danger when their head goes all the way into the flowers. The nectar, however, is rich and plentiful. Where other flowers spread their pollen in small amounts on a hummingbird's bill, a ruby-throated hummingbird may nearly disappear into the flower of a trumpet vine and reappear with its head covered by grains of pollen.

Other plants recommended for people living east of the Mississippi include hollyhock, spider flower, sweet William, foxglove, gladiolus, butterfly weed, Indian paintbrush, bleeding heart, cardinal flower, morning glory, and lantana. It's possible to have good luck with red impatiens, but only late in the season when it has attained its full growth. In the West, many of these same flowers may be grown, but there are also some western specialties such as desert honeysuckle, Texas olive, Mexican bush sage, ocotillo, bottlebrush, shrimp plant, and century plant. Western gardeners have the advantage of living where more than one kind of hummingbird may visit their plantings, especially if they live in Arizona or southern California.

Aside from choosing colors that attract hummingbirds, a gardener should try to lure them by planting a mixture of tubular or trumpet shaped flowers that bloom at different times of the year.

Desert honeysuckle, ocotillo, bottlebrush, and shrimp plant are some of the flowers favored by western hummingbirds. This broadtailed hummingbird is savoring a blossom in Madera Canyon, Arizona.

UNITED STATES HUMMINGBIRDS

Sixteen different species of hummingbird breed regularly in the United States.

Allen's Hummingbird

This small hummingbird, 3 to 3.5 inches (7.6–8.9 centimeters), is seldom found very far from the Pacific coast of California and Southern Oregon. It has a shiny green and orange back and a scarlet gorget; in most plumages it resembles the more widely distributed rufous hummingbird.

Anna's Hummingbird

A medium-sized species, 3.5 to 4 inches (8.9–10 centimeters), this is found in California and the desert southwest through

LEFT: Anna's hummingbird

Arizona and southern New Mexico as far east as Big Bend National Park in Texas. It is characterized by red iridescent feathers that cover the gorget and most of the head.

Berylline Hummingbird *(not pictured)*

Rarely seen, this medium-sized hummingbird is green with brownish highlights on the wings. In the United States it breeds only in the mountains of southeastern Arizona.

Black-chinned Hummingbird

A medium-sized hummingbird widely distributed and frequently seen throughout the desert and mountain West as far north as the Canadian border, it has also been an occasional visitor to most southeastern states. It has a green back and an iridescent gorget that varies from black to deep purple depending on lighting conditions.

*Allen's
hummingbird*

*FOLLOWING PAGE:
Black-chinned
hummingbird*

*Broad-billed
hummingbird*

Blue-throated Hummingbird

With a length of 5 inches (12.7 centimeters), this is one of the two largest U.S. hummingbirds. Its range is limited to southeastern Arizona and the Big Bend in Texas, but it is relatively easy to observe in those areas. It has a distinctive light blue gorget, white streaks at and below the eye, a greenish back, and a grayish breast.

Broad-billed Hummingbird

Like the blue-throated, this medium-sized species is found only in southeastern Arizona and the Big Bend. As its name implies, its bill is noticeably wide, especially at the base. It is a mostly green bird with a blue gorget.

Broad-tailed Hummongbird

This medium-sized hummingbird is abundant through much of the Rockies north to central Wyoming and southern Idaho. Along with the black-chinned, it is the bird most frequently seen at feeders in Colorado and New Mexico. It has generally green plumage with a bright red gorget and resembles the eastern ruby-throated hummingbird.

Broad-tailed hummingbird

Blue-throated hummingbird

59

Buff-bellied Hummingbvird

A medium-sized to largish bird with a noticeably down-curved bill, this species occurs along the Gulf Coast as far east as the Florida panhandle, but is most easily observed in southern Texas. It has a shiny green gorget, a buff breast, and a green back.

Calliope Hummingbird

With a length of 2 1/2 to 3 1/4 inches (6.4–8.2 centimeters), this is the smallest American hummingbird. It has a fairly wide distribution through the mountains and deserts west of the Rockies and north to Canada, and it migrates through the Rockies. It has a green back and a distinctive red gorget in which separate feathers are visible.

Costa's Hummingbird

This small hummingbird lives in the driest areas of southern California, Nevada, and Arizona. It is mostly dull green with a purple gorget that extends well down the sides of the chest.

Buff-bellied hummingbird

ABOVE: *Calliope hummingbird*

RIGHT: *Costa's hummingbird*

Lucifer Hummingbird

A medium-sized species with a curved bill, a forked tail, and a long violet gorget, it is found close to the Mexican border in southeastern Arizona, New Mexico, and southwestern Texas.

Magnificent Hummingbird

One of the largest North American species, this is another eastern Arizona hummingbird, but its range reaches to the northern part of the state and also encompasses much of western New Mexico. It has a green back, a purple crown, and a brilliant green gorget.

Ruby-throated Hummingbird

This medium-sized species is widely distributed and reasonably abundant throughout the eastern United States and southern Canada, where it is the only regularly occurring hummingbird. It has a green back, a white breast, and a bright red gorget.

ABOVE:
Lucifer humming-bird

Magnificent hummingbird

LEFT: Ruby-throated hummingbird

63

Rufous Hummingbird
With the northernmost range of any hummingbird species, this medium-sized bird summers from Oregon north through British Columbia and Alaska to about the sixtieth parallel. Its back and head are rust colored and its throat is bright red.

Violet-crowned Hummingbird
This large Mexican species, whose range barely enters the United States at the border between Arizona and New Mexico, has a greenish back, and a violet head, and its breast and throat are entirely white with no distinctive gorget.

White-eared Hummingbird
A medium-sized hummingbird found in the United States only in the extreme southeastern corner of Arizona, it has a purple head and throat, a green chest, and a distinctive white eye stripe.

ABOVE:
Rufous hummingbird

White-eared hummingbird

RIGHT: *Violet-crowned hummingbird*

Traveling to Observe Hummingbirds

People interested in viewing more species of hummingbirds than those they can attract to their own yards are fortunate in that many good places to see hummingbirds are also attractive vacation destinations. So-called "hummingbird hotspots" in the United States are located in the Southwest, particularly in southeastern Arizona, where it is sometimes possible to see as many as ten species in a day, and in southern California. In other areas, such as the Colorado Rockies, large numbers of hummingbirds may be found, but only a couple of species, namely the black-chinned and the broad-tailed, will usually be represented. A few places, like the Sable Palm Grove sanctuary in Brownsville, Texas, are known for hosting one species otherwise difficult to find, in this case the buff-breasted hummingbird.

Outside the United States, people taking Caribbean cruises will find hummingbirds on most islands, although even large islands like Puerto Rico and Jamaica have only three or four species. Trinidad and Tobago are the exception, with seventeen species, and Jamaica is the home of the streamertail, one of the most spectacular hummingbirds. The mainland countries of Latin America from Costa Rica south through Peru and Brazil all are home to more than fifty kinds of hummingbirds.

In this whole region, finding hummingbirds is not difficult; what poses the problem is trying to sort them out. Their small size, rapid movement, and seemingly changeable coloring can make species identification an intimidating challenge. There are two ways of overcoming this problem when birding in an unfamiliar region. The first is to go to a place where hummingbird feeders abound and are

One of the rewards of traveling to the tropics to observe hummingbirds is the chance to see such magnificent creatures as this rufous-breasted hermit in French Guyana.

kept freshly filled, places like the Monteverde Reserve in Costa Rica. Find a comfortable place to sit (often the people who maintain the feeders provide lawn chairs or benches), and watch until you become familiar with the local hummingbird population. Before long you will feel comfortable identifying species that visit the feeders frequently, and soon you will be able to begin identifying those appearing only sporadically. Visitors to Monteverde can learn to recognize eight or ten species in an hour or so.

A second and more rewarding approach is to go birding with a local resident who knows both where to find and how to identify species in his or her neighborhood. In Peru I had the privilege of being led through some excellent hummingbird habitat near Macchu Picchu by a grandmotherly Peruvian guide who simply adored hummingbirds. With her help I enjoyed memorable views of seven species during a walk of

In many places in Latin America, the variety of hummingbird species is so abundant, it is often difficult to identify them all. Here is seen a male purple-throated mountain-gem in Costa Rica's tropical cloud forest.

A broad-billed hummingbird in flight. These birds can be seen by travelers to southeastern Arizona and the Big Bend in south-western Texas.

about an hour. The day before, birding the same area on my own, I had only been able to come up with a confident identification for a single species, and I had overlooked some nearby flowering trees where hummingbirds abounded.

Prospects

Hummingbird population trends are very difficult to assess. It seems reasonable to assume that the destruction of rain forests in South and Central America, which has done serious damage to many other types of birds, has also negatively affected hummingbirds. But it is not known which species have been most affected and how serious the damage has been. In the United States hummingbirds, unlike many other groups of birds, do not seem to have suffered much from human population growth and the development of modern technology. They are, of course, vulnerable to high concentrations of pesticides on flowering plants, something gardeners should remember. For the most

do not seem to be decreasing. Most of the rarer North American hummingbirds are scarce only because Arizona or Texas represent the extreme northern edge of their ranges. They are neither rare nor endangered in Mexico and Central America.

Whether you find them in remote, exotic places or in the familiar surroundings of your own back yard, the joy of observing and studying hummingbirds is deeply rewarding and matches few other experiences humans can have in their encounter with the natural world.

Hummingbirds like this blue-tailed sylph were once killed by the thousands so their feathers could be used as fashion accessories. Today, this practice has ended and large-scale extinction of species is not imminent.

part, however, they visit plants other than those grown agriculturally. They frequent flowers and shrubs grown ornamentally, ones that usually do not receive heavy doses of pesticides. As the suburbs have expanded, more and more ornamental plants have been introduced, a boon for the hummingbird population.

The prominent North American species such as the rufous, the black-chinned, the calliope, the broad-tailed, and the ruby-throated seem to have stable populations, and their ranges

The giant hummingbird, found in South America's Andes Mountains, measures about 8 inches (20.03 cm) long. It is the largest of all hummingbirds, The smallest is the Cuban bee hummingbird, with a length of only 2 1/4 inches (5.7 cm).

A long-tailed hermit calls to females from his song perch at a lek site. The males of certain tropical species often join together to form singing choruses, or leks, in their attempt to attract females.

Developments in nature photography, along with increased travel opportunities, have made it possible for even the armchair naturalist to view such beauties as this Brazilian violet-capped wood nymph.

INDEX

*Page numbers in **bold-face** type indicate photo captions.*